# To Heal the Broken Heart

# To Heal the Broken Heart
## Prayers, Poems and Art, from the Heart

### Rev. Dr. Gina Rose Halpern

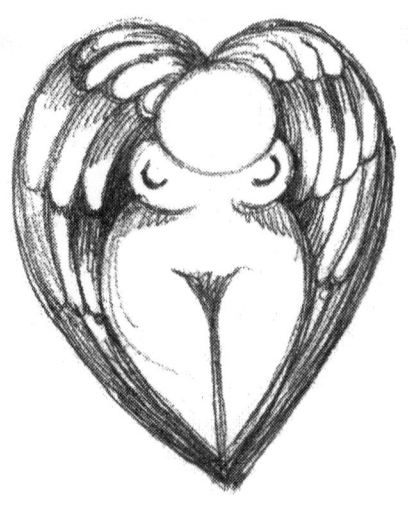

the apocryphile press
BERKELEY, CA
www.apocryphile.org

apocryphile press
BERKELEY, CA

Apocryphile Press
1700 Shattuck Ave #81
Berkeley, CA 94709
www.apocryphile.org

First Apocryphile Press edition, 2006.
ISBN 0-9771461-4-6

Book Design: Liz Kalloch
Editorial: Tristy Taylor,
Readers: Charles Michael Burack, Ph.D.,
Rabbi Michael Ziegler,
Rev. Jeremy Taylor

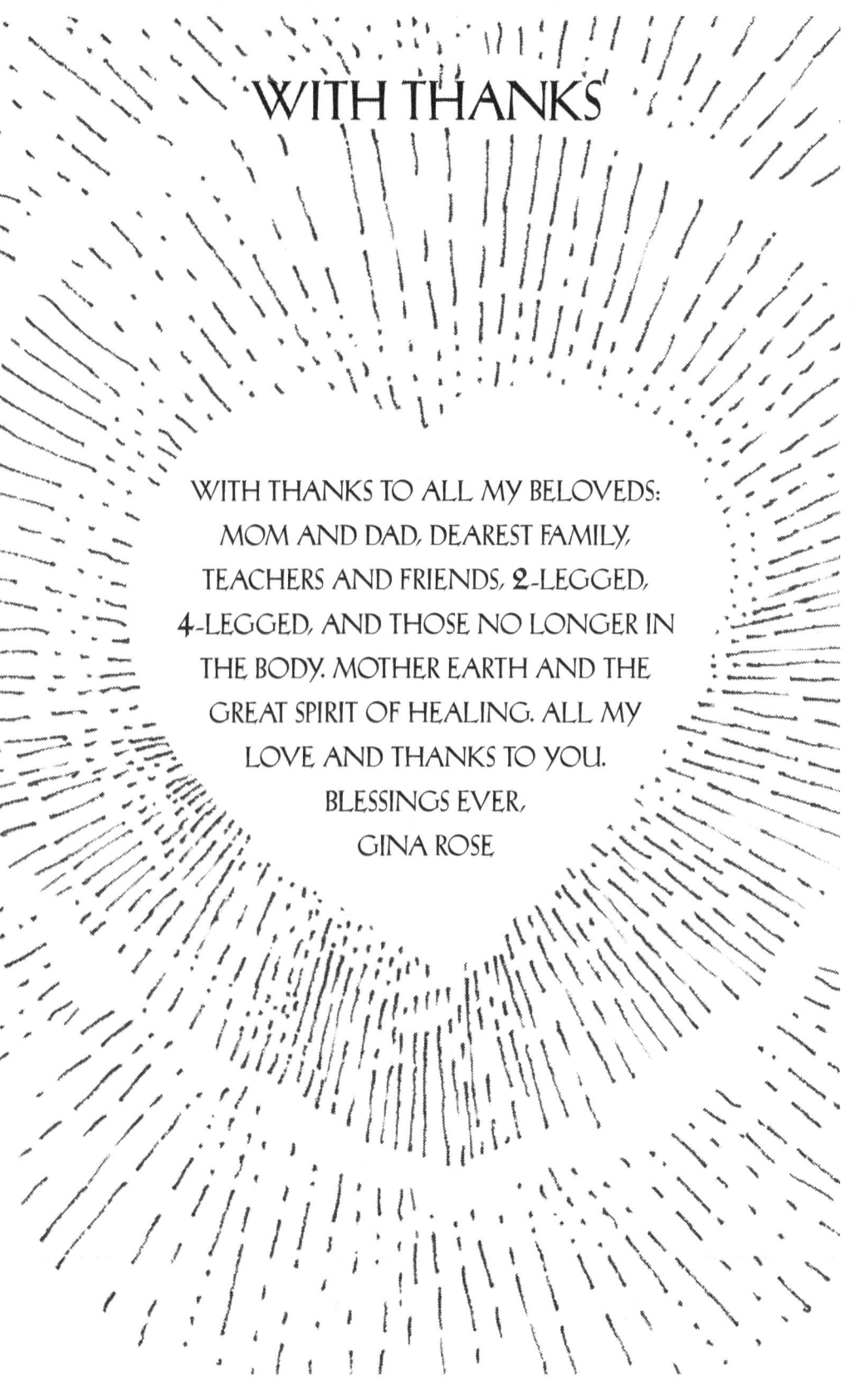

# WITH THANKS

WITH THANKS TO ALL MY BELOVEDS:
MOM AND DAD, DEAREST FAMILY,
TEACHERS AND FRIENDS, 2-LEGGED,
4-LEGGED, AND THOSE NO LONGER IN
THE BODY. MOTHER EARTH AND THE
GREAT SPIRIT OF HEALING. ALL MY
LOVE AND THANKS TO YOU.
BLESSINGS EVER,
GINA ROSE

# CONTENTS

# Meditations for the Heart     117

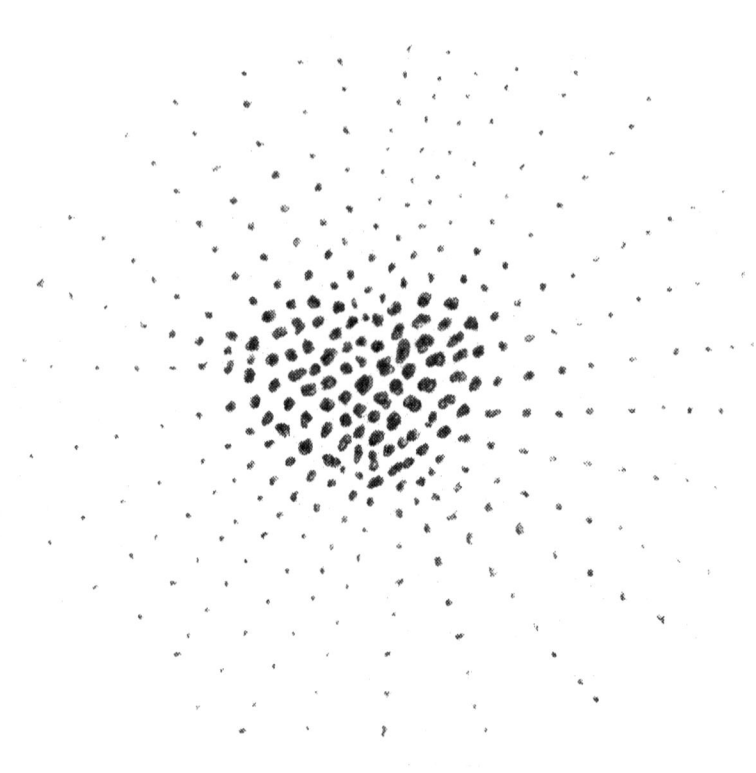

ho among us has not had a broken heart? Our hearts can be emotionally broken, by losing a lover, a parent, a child, a home or even a pet. The heart can be spiritually broken by the loss of faith or personal ideals. The heart can be physically broken, through birth defects, illness and heart disease. The actual physical pumping of the heart can be damaged to the point of death, by the stress from emotional and spiritual heartbreak, the absence of love, and the loss of intimacy and spiritual connection.

If you are reading these pages, chances are you have suffered or are suffering from some kind of heartbreak in your own life, or you are concerned for someone dear to you. We encourage you to breathe deeply, be gentle with yourself and read on. In the book written by Dean Ornish, M.D., entitled, Love and Survival, Dr. Ornish explores the intimate links between the physical breakdown of the heart and relates it to the sense of separation, loss and isolation we all go through in our lives. His book shows the inherent healing possibilities in support from friends and family, as well as the concept of interdependence and connection between all people. Ornish, a cardiologist, sees immense healing possible for all of us, through the love and spirit accessible to us in our everyday lives. In this book *To Heal the Broken Heart*, I explore the healing potentials of creativity, prayer, humor and nature which have been of value to me in my own healing and which I have witnessed as beneficial to those I work with.

I am an Interfaith minister and direct The Chaplaincy Institute for Arts and Interfaith Ministries. We train interfaith chaplains and ministers to work in healthcare, hospice and communities using the arts as a method of spiritual and pastoral care. In my private practice as minister, chaplain and spiritual teacher I have sung for the dying and been a shoulder for the tears of the grieving.

On my path, I have been guided by Buddha, the Jewish Scriptures, Mohammed, Jesus, Quan Yin, Mother Nature, Santa Claus, my cat and my own encounter with illness. When I reached my young adulthood, my spiritual path called me into the desert and on this new path, I had many "dark nights of the soul." Much like Moses, I surrendered to the call of the burning bush and I took off my shoes, tearing open my ribs, and yelling to God to bring the fire inside my heart.

In my ancestry, my grandfather died of heart disease and my father and brother who both have large and feeling hearts, have high blood pressure. Like myself, all of the men in my family have intense creativity, passion, and compassion in their hearts, and I think that is why we suffer from "broken hearts" which we work to mend in every possible way, including exercise, diet, art and music, meditation and nature.

When I turned 50 the "accelerator switch" on my heart wore out and the defective valve that I was born with began to propel my heart rate up to 200 beats per minute, I was completely perplexed. I wondered if I had gotten enough sleep, or if I had not eaten enough lunch that day. As a child of the era of psychology, I assumed my illness was all in my head. When my heart was beating so quickly, I felt like I was running an internal marathon. It left me too exhausted to lift a cup off the counter and too sad to cry. This was the final step in surrendering to the power of my body and my heart.

As my illness progressed, I had to give up driving. The stress of traffic often caused my heart to begin racing, so I parked my car in the driveway and did not step into it for months. One morning, I tried to drive myself to the doctor only to discover that the battery was dead. I realized that this was a perfect metaphor for the way my body felt.

At this point, I entered a depression so vast that the night sky seemed smaller than the hole inside my soul. I continued breathing but my life seemed to be nothing but death. I felt overwhelmed by the constant confrontation of sorrow, loneliness and the unanswered questions of my life and the life of the world. I lost my connection to God in this sea of questions. I continued to pray but felt alone in the universe.

One night my heart was racing and the medication I was taking did nothing to help. I ended up in the emergency room.

My faulty heart valve was resistant to all medical measures. They hooked me up to an IV and told me they were going to give me a medication that would stop my heart and then re-boot it, like a computer. Hopefully, this procedure would start my heart at a regular speed. They gave me the medication, and I asked the doctor to hold my hand. He held my pinkie finger because everything else was attached to various machines. I felt the medication taking effect. It felt like I was falling backwards, weightless in an immense velvety darkness. It felt like falling into the arms of the universe. I felt united with the energetic presence of infinite space. I did not "go towards the light," as many describe doing. Instead, I fell slowly and gently into a peaceful and restful darkness. The cosmos was pulling me and I had no desire to return to my body from this near-death experience.

It felt like I had fallen into the void of enlightenment that the Buddhists always seek in meditation. I felt that I had surrendered into the peace beyond all understanding of the Christian Gospels, or the all encompassing, primal and divine Creator of the Hebrew Bible. When the surgery to correct my heart problem (diagnosed as Tachycardia) was completed, and it was time to return to my physical body, I did not want to leave this place of quiet connection and deep peace.

Much time has passed since my illness and surgery, and I realize that I have managed to return to the land of the living with some of that contentment and peace that I encountered in my near death experience.

I can sustain this sense of peace through prayer, meditation, rest, humor, long sessions of ministry from my cat, and creative activities all of which have become part of my continued journey towards health, wholeness and connection to the Holy. I seem to have been sent back into the world to share what I have learned of the velvety singing peace of death and the possibility of healing the heart.

Part of the healing has been to mend the split between the intellectual need to understand existence and the hearts' desire to flow into existence, and experience the knowing that the intimate and the universal are one.

Philosophical and rational thought tells us that there is a veil between the worlds of our dreams and the waking world, as well as between life and death. I have come to believe that at any given moment of our lives we are all moving back and forth over the threshold between intellect and the accepting, loving nature of the heart. This incarnate life is a dance with death and the sense of ultimate being. This waltz of acceptance can be a passionate dance with a lot of peace, that brings the possibility of healing. The rhythm of our dance of life is the rhythm of the heartbeat.

During my illness and recovery, I began keeping a journal as a spiritual practice and I continue to use it to this day. Dr Stephen Sinatra, M.D. said in his book *Heartbreak and Heart Disease: A Mind Body Prescription for Healing the Heart*: "Writing a journal is one of the best ways to deepen your connection with yourself and keep yourself on a spiritual path."[1]

My journal is the home of my spirituality and creativity. I have made a spiritual practice of drawing a heart that reflects the condition of my

I. Pg. 228, Sinatra, S, M.D. (1996) *Heartbreak & Heart Disease: A Mind/Body Prescription for Healing the Heart*, New Canaan, CT: Keats Publishing, INC.

own physical, emotional and spiritual heart each night. Then I write a corresponding prayer. First comes the drawing and then comes the prayer. This is an organic process of the heart leading the mind. Buddhists would call these images "spontaneous arising." These images are not preplanned, but instead rise out of the direct experience of the moment.

As an Interfaith Minister and pilgrim on the spiritual path, I have explored many of the world's faith traditions and have been inspired by the beauty and wisdom of spiritual literature. I am a practicing Jewish/Christian/Buddhist/Artist with mystical inclinations. World scripture, poetry, art, and music inform and inspire me. I usually begin my prayers and journal entries with an invocation to the Divine Source, drawn from my love of the *Song of Songs* and the *Psalms* of David from the Hebrew Bible, as well as the work of the Sufi poet Rumi. As an Interfaith Minister, I call this Source by many different names. I call to God, the Beloved, and the Cultivator of my Soul, just to name a few. I find that addressing the Source in this way, also keeps me attuned to the many facets of Spirit.

> In waking life and dreams, my heart has been infused with flames and fireworks. I have surrendered to the burning bush. I took off my shoes and tore open my ribs and finally called the fire inside my heart.
>
> —Gina Rose Halpern

In the dark sorrow of the broken heart, there is a spark of spirit we all carry from the fires of suffering. This is the spark of healing and divine illumination. This spark ignites our imaginations and fires our ability to make art, to compose music, and to invent new forms of expression so that we can become whole. This process of inquiry, yearning and discovery forms the basis of my journal-keeping and my spiritual practice. This journey of the heart forms the basis for this book.

Creative expression of thoughts and feelings is a powerful vehicle for healing. Without this outward creative expression the nature of suffering and the experience of fear remain internalized and can ultimately become destructive, manifesting as illness. I personally have made a sojourn into the netherworld of illness, and have experienced a literal "broken heart." I traveled into death and made the journey back again into life. The life I now lead has been greatly altered by this human pilgrimage. The prayers and poems that I offer to you in this book, chart my healing and the understandings gained through the adventures with my broken heart.

I now see that the experience with my injured heart valve has been my doorway to vulnerability and love, and is a place of attention, intention and healing.

The losses in my life and my illness have brought me to this great question: **do we choose our illness and suffering or does it choose us?**

Each time we approach the nature of suffering we can discover new levels of understanding and truth. It seems the enigma of grace and compassion gained through suffering, is only achieved through the actual suffering itself. Our ability to grow and to heal corresponds to our ability to keep our hearts open to this great, fierce teacher of suffering, instead of shutting down in the face of pain.

Over the years working as an artist, teacher and minister I have been touched by the phenomenological dimensions, of life, death, prayer and healing. I am awed, and humbled by the great mystery and power of these experiences.

There is a wonderful reassurance to be found in the new scientific proof that places the world of spirit in a context of statistical evidence. In Dr. Larry Dossey's books *Prayer is Good Medicine*, and *Healing Words*, he cites study after study that record the positive outcomes for patients that have been prayed for regardless of faith traditions, or personal belief. This scientific evidence of the healing power of prayer does not diminish the mystery. Instead it grounds it and makes it more accessible to both believers and non-believers alike.

One of the outcomes of a regular spiritual practice is to accept, and maybe even love, the nature of change. By not grasping each moment or becoming angry at life when it doesn't give us what we want, we can move into a state of flexibility and peace. Unfortunately for most of us this is easier said than done. Thich Nhat Hanh, the great Vietnamese monk states in his book *Living Buddha, Living Christ.*

I try to live my life with awareness and appreciation of what is currently in my perceived reality and the inevitability of change which can cause suffering.

Buddhists believe that we have one life and many bodies. My own experience seems to be that we have one body and many lives. Much to my amazement, I am still walking around on this planet in the relatively recognizable, though altered form of Gina Rose Halpern. I have experienced re-incarnation, and yet I have stayed in this one body. In this one life, my broken heart experienced healing and rebirth. With great thanks and blessings, I offer my heart to you in the form of my drawings, prayers and poems in this book. May my reflections help you on your journey to heal your broken heart.

Throughout the book we have provided hearts with questions for you to reflect upon or draw your own heart in response to the images on the page. How to heal the broken heart is a question we all ask. My prayer is that this book will be a companion for you on your journey towards healing.

I come to you
    With my heart
        In my hand
            It is a gift I offer,
                Please accept.

Gina Rose Halpern

# The Broken Heart

"Where do you place your self
On the map of the soul
Have you ever held
Your heart hostage in
The great abyss?"

# Heart Like the Bermuda Triangle

Where do you place your self,
On the map of the soul?
Have you ever held your heart hostage in
The great abyss?

My Heart is like the Bermuda Triangle
posted with a sign that says:
"GIVE UP HOPE,
ALL YE WHO ENTER HERE!"

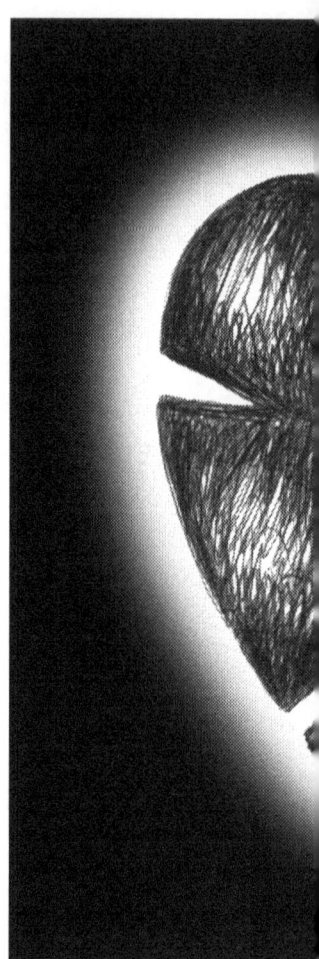

My heart has been a vortex of
    mysterious losses and disappearances.

I would love to blame it all on you,
    who ever you are
        but,
the truth is, blame does not help.

My heart has felt like
Hiroshima.
    I would like to blame you
    for dropping the bomb,
    when you said
        you did not love me.

But the truth is,
    you just said the words.
    I dropped the bomb on
myself.
    A direct hit
    from head to heart,
    turning all to ash.
        And now in this
        wasteland of being,
        I wonder if life
        will ever be restored?

In the vast emptiness of

    the internal void,

    a small flame sputtered

    over the stream of tears.


I make a pilgrimage

    to this miraculous juncture

    fire over water.

I lay myself upon the altar

    and in a whisper I say,

    "Oh spark of life,

    allow me to venerate

    the possibility of your existence

    in the heart of the

    Bermuda Triangle."

# Insomnia Prayer
## 2 am: "Oh God, come to me"

I am afraid.
My dreams are full of murder.
   Who am I killing?
My perfectionism.
My old habits and beliefs.
I am shooting out the parts of me that
      have been so entrenched
      in ideas of unworthiness,
that only by proving and
improving myself,
might I finally be acceptable
to receive the treasures
that have been hidden.


We are digging up the treasure in
the garden.
I can't believe that I deserve the gifts.

The treasure of love,
the abundant life.
It is illegal to have it.
I am killing my old illusions
and assumptions.
The treasure is in me.

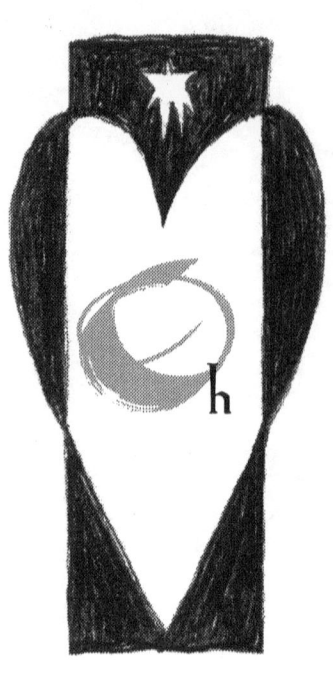

# Oh, Comfort in Sorrow, Oh, Comfort of Prayer

In my anger and grieving
you heard me.
In my pain and loneliness
you touched me.
You have given me
a most treasured reality.
In my own back yard
you taught me
to be still and breathe,
while my tears
flowed into the earth.
For this
I give thanks.

# Prayer For A Suffering Friend

I watch you navigate your pain

You make it seem as easy as a cruise,

Under sail, between islands,

At the changing tide.

Any one who has navigated through

The shoals of sorrow

Knows how difficult the journey is.


I am in awe,

You travel with such grace

I wish that I could pray:

"Lord, let me take the pain

For this friend of mine."

But,

Lord forgive me,

I am afraid of the suffering.

But,

Maybe if I said give me her pain for

Just one hour

I could bear the pain.
Knowing it would be finite
And not infinite.
Maybe I could take the pain for
Longer still.

And God, if you could help me
To really listen
To the things
I don't really want to hear,
Because I know sometimes
Shared pain is easier,
It can turn a solitary walk
Into a dance.

# Heal the Shame

I am ashamed,
Please hear my confession
And accept my prayer.
Please accept me,
In my fear and humanity.

I am not a Saint!!
I get angry at the unfairness
And, I get afraid of my anger.
Please,
Give me the courage
To rant and rave
So that the ears of heaven
Would open to the cries
Ease the Pain
Please.

Please, heal the shame and
Ease the Pain.

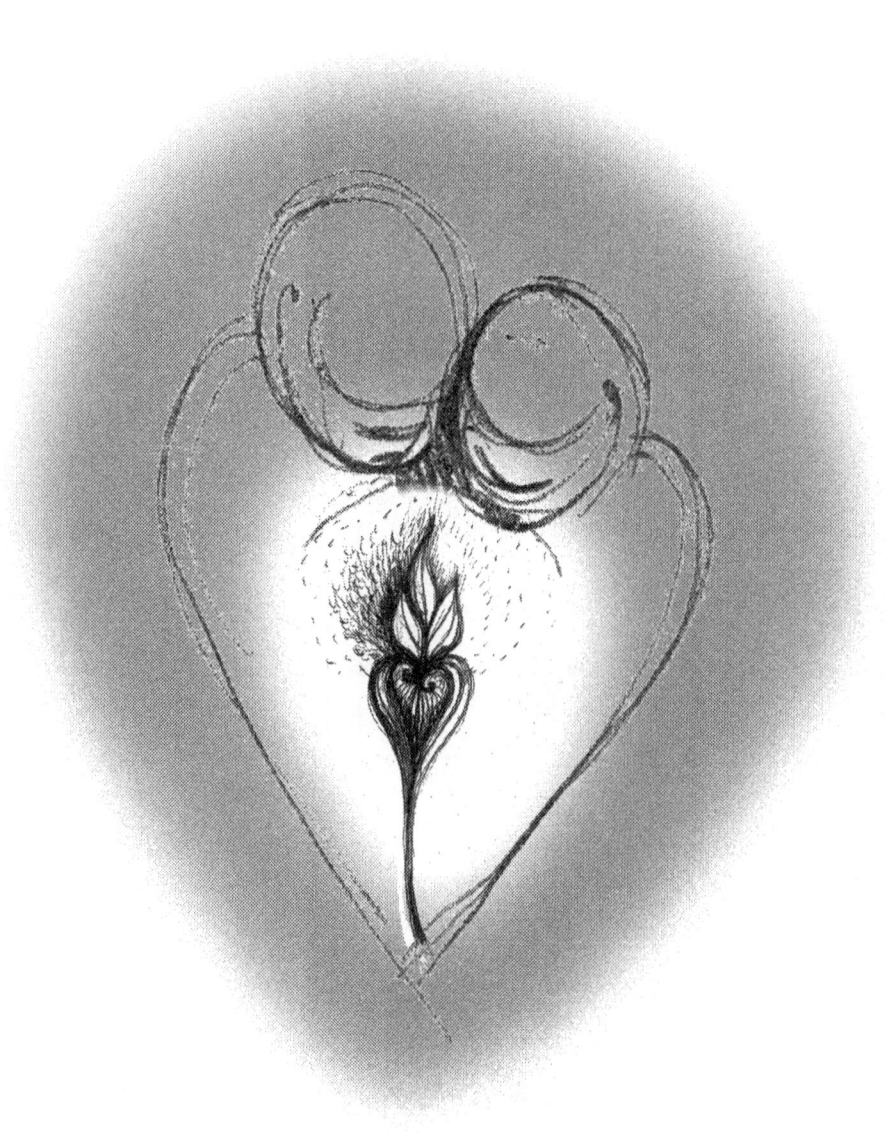

# Protector of the Heart Garden

I am frightened
in my vulnerability.

I am frightened by the fluttering
    uneven beating of my heart.

I am frightened by change.
    I invoke your quiet presence.

As I send out tentative tendrils
    of feeling,
I beg you
    to support my tenderness.

Protect me against those who would
    eat me up
(not out of vicious intent),
    even the dear/deer,

their soft lips
nibble new buds.
Garden my soul
and tend me
gently.

Who are you waiting for?

# Healing the Broken Heart

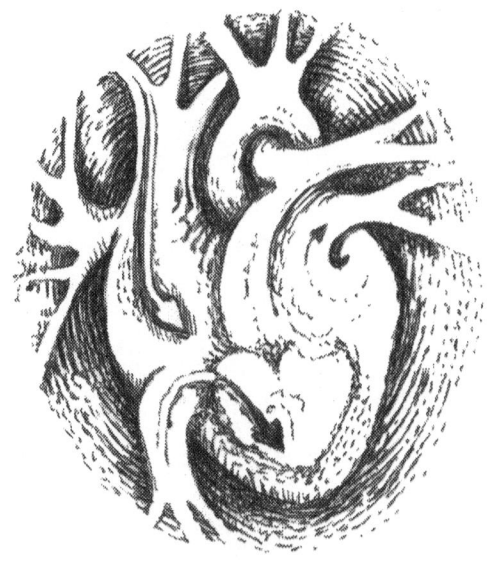

"Let's celebrate your incarnation
With salmon and wine
And hope."

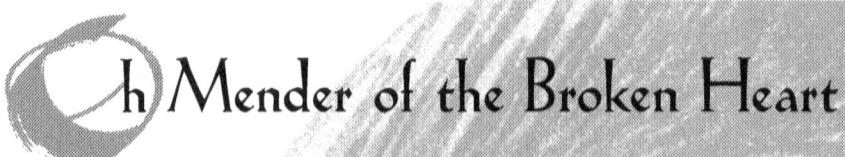

# Oh Mender of the Broken Heart

My heart is feeling
a spaciousness
as if the edges of constriction
had fallen away.

I am released by permission
into feeling and emotion.

I give thanks
for the moment
on this perfect morning.

Where my body
and the soft dog ear
and the sound of water
and the blue sky
and the sparkling light
awoke.

We're not distinct entities
no I
no thou
just Is.

# Miracles of the Breath
# Miracles of the Heart

My prayers have become so simple.

They are not for some spicy lover.

My prayers have become quiet and constant.

They are prayers for stillness and good sleep.

Thanksgiving for the soft fur of my cat,

    each stroke from head to tail

    is a rosary of loving.

Thanks for the remembrance

    with each breath,

    each inhalation, each exhalation,

    that there is a second of total quiet

    between the in and the out.

And in this quiet there is a gentle and profound

    intimation of death,

    or a remembrance of time before birth.

That nano-second is a reminder of the peace

    that lies beyond the simple exercise of breathing.

Raise the eyebrows slightly,

    flare the nostrils to receive

the incoming air.
Lift the corners of the mouth.
Smile, because the heart knows
   the miracle of how to keep its rhythm
   and its song.
Listen.
Let the breath drop into the chest.
Each breath is a comet falling to earth
   rest between the falling stars.
Picture yourself
   sitting at the bottom of the breath
   warming your hands over the divine spark.
The radiating star of breath
   that resides within you.
Look out through your ribcage,
   like the branches
   of a rhododendron forest,
   the bark shining in the high altitude
   moonlight.
Know these are the moments
   when the veil between the worlds
   is the space of a heartbeat
   and thin enough to breathe through.

# WHoly Beloved,
## I am coming to believe

The you that resides in me

    loves me warmly, and solidly

      without doubt.

I am learning to trust.

There is such comfort

    in that kind of love

    that my skin relaxes.

      The me that says NO to love

      is weeping on the counter,

Calling myself an ugly fool
and waiting for
abandonment and betrayal.
You, in me are saying
"Be patient, and trust.
I am knocking at the door."
I say:   "Welcome, come in and eat,
I've set the table . . .


Let's celebrate your incarnation
with salmon
and wine
and hope."

# Night Gratitude

I give thanks for

    the rich body of this night

    that calls me to sing a brief

    love song to the dipper,

    pouring syrup over

    the eastern hills and mooing cows.

Beloved, I can feel your

    surrounding nature wrapping

    each strand of hair

    with electric concentration

    that draws the light of the stars

    to our eyes

    as memories from far away.

Is what I see of Orion's belt

    hunting for me above my home

    an illusion?

    Or the hope of being found?

Call me out to sit with you

as you fill me to the brim

with your exquisite concertos

of silence and moonlight.

# Rainy Night Prayer

I am so tired.

I leave my feet by the door next to my shoes.

Thank you

For the rain soaking into the earth,

This Friday night rain is a Sabbath blessing.

This rain is watering the acts of faith.

The acts of faith are hidden under ground.

The acts of faith are buried treasures named:

Salmon Petal Tulip bulbs,
Stargazer Lilies,
Asian Bearded Iris,
And Bleeding Hearts.

On this rainy night,
I allow myself to burrow into my soft bed.
I hibernate with rabbits and bears.

The rain quiets my heart.
I sleep, dreaming of the ark
Of the old and new covenant.
I dream of fertile compost piles
In the middle of my floor.
I dream of emerging teachers
I have yet to meet.

Rainy nights are essential for
Percolating the unrevealed Foliage of the heart.

Thank you for this rainy night.

# Heart like a Toaster

What is your heart like?
In seventh grade we learned about
    the power of metaphor
      to describe the indescribable.
Is your heart like a toaster?
Sometimes burning the toast?
Sometimes underdone?

I have learned about toasters.
To receive the perfect piece of toast
     you must give the toaster perfect attention.


Is your heart like the broken radiator
     and water pump in my Toyota?
Are you safe on the flats
     but overheat with any effort of exertion?
Do hills send you boiling over?


How can I know your heart if you don't tell me
     in a metaphor,
     and I don't know how to ask?
Tell me what your heart is like.

# imple Gifts

I am blessed with
Sleep, quiet,
Food, and the
Movements of your
Hands, my hands
Comfort, beauty
Sweetness.
For these I give thanks.
What else is there
But these simple gifts?
The illustrated truths of life.

Contentment is underrated.
It is a gift of the Spirit.
The aaah of Amen
At the end of
Prayer.

# More Than Anatomy

With gratitude, I send my appreciation to my heart,
  To this bundle of muscle and flesh
  That carries the fresh blood
  Through this dense body
  To my denser mind.

But oh my bloody blob of tissue,
  You are more than this simple anatomy!
You are the origin of every heart-felt kiss.
The bliss of loving
  lounges in the playroom and the bed chamber
  of your complex being.
Another chamber is the chapel
  of my loneliness and grief.
Heartbreak is the burnt offering
  on the altar.
The thief of youth sits like the couch-potato it is,
  watching romantic re-runs of old sad stories,
  blocking arteries with old sorrows
  and chocolate.

In the great chamber

    where oxygen charges and changes

    every cell into life

    here is a celebration with a rhythm and blues band,

    beating out a soulful and even harmony.


I won't say my heart never missed a beat.

I can say, with appreciation

    that this morning I planted pale pink cyclamen

    with heart shaped leaves

    and black eyed susans.

When I rested, leaning on the shovel

    to watch a hummingbird sipping

    at the butterfly bush,

    the handle of the spade was pressed

    up under my breast.

    I could feel the lub-dubbing of my heart

    singing me into a gentle partner dance,

    a dance of smooth-pulsing appreciation,

    a dance of gratitude.

Do you defend your heart?

# Happy Heart

"YES!
Let the corners of your mouth rise up
And the heart will follow
YES, YES."

# For the Blessing of Laughter

There is a gift that comes to the heart

To tickle each cell into life.

Do not underestimate the healing power

    Of giggle,

    Of guffaw.

The belly laugh that splits the side

    Also splits the heart,

And in this opening love flows in,

Delight pours through arteries,

Like the river from the source.

YES!
Let the corners of your mouth rise up
And the heart will follow.
YES, YES!

# Heart Soup

With praise and thanks I offer this recipe
    for heart and hearty soup.
Now as the days are shorter,
the long and chilly nights give me the craving
for warm and cozy soup.

This is the food which feeds the hungry body and the soul:
6 Parts Sliced yams, sweet potato or pumpkin,
    cut into little pieces while remembering:
Swimming in the Bay with my laughing parents
    the nieces with their curling hair.
Walking in the woods with my brother and his son.

2 cups of onions chopped and mixed with tears
    of lost love flavoring the broth with salt.

1 cup golden raisins inhaling the aroma
    of the sun that dried them,
    the sun that now wrinkles my skin.
    may I age
    sweet and useful like a raisin to the soup.

1 hand full of seasonal herbs
      that will die in the first frost
      but return in the spring


3 cups of orange juice
      poured from a blue cup given by an old friend.


These ingredients I will simmer on the stove
      smelling the fragrant aroma
      as I lie in the couch
      with my cat on my chest
      and read a novel of true love
      and a psalm of praise.
            When we speak of needing hearty soup
                  the ingredients may differ
                        but the heart provides the
                        nourishment.
                              Cook until everything is soft.

# Strong Heart
# Rx for Healing

Strong Heart,

Rx for Healing,

Meditation, medication and motivation,

　All may be needed.

Mix with the company of others

　So that we don't loose

　Ourselves to the sorrow

　Of loneliness.

Suffering can become a snob to joy.

Large doses of laughter in every form

　Are needed.

　Big dogs, small children,

　Stupid movies,

　Prescription chocolate in moderate doses.

Men and women,

　Both will do well to follow these

　Recommendations,

Remember to complete the course of treatment

To alleviate painful symptoms

So that peace and health may be restored.

# Heart like a Hedgehog

for Rayhanna

My heart is like an African Pigmy Hedgehog.
If you come too close,
If you move too fast,
I roll into a ball and I show you my spikes.
Frighten me and I become a thorny brush.

My Goddaughter loves her African Pigmy Hedgehog.
She holds this quivering ball of spines
With gloves on her hands and croons to it
Until it pokes out a tender nose and two bright eyes.
Her face lights up with devotion.
Her hedgehog is the same size as my heart
Weighing about one pound.

How do hedgehogs fall in love?
Slowly and gently.

# Teach This Silly Body To Dance

Oh Source Of Creation,
You who created the Pelican
    And the Blue Footed Boobie,
    And giraffe,
    I Beg you, teach this silly body to dance.
Let this round belly laugh
    Let these stiff limbs flex
    Teach this body to dance!

Let us not be ashamed of
    Our shapes
    And our forms,
    Our Curves and
    Our colors.

Teach us to see ourselves
    As no less wondrous than
    Toucans
    And Tigers
    And Ring Tailed Lemurs.

Help us to find delight in our soft fur.
Teach us to throw back our heads
    And howl at the moon
    Without shame.

Let us praise these bodies that carry us
    To the edge of the world
    Where we can watch the sun
    Kiss the ocean in a passion
    Of unashamed pinkness.

Oh source of Creation
    Teach this silly body to dance.
And when we are tired teach
Us to lie down and rest and dream.
So that we may dance again
    Tomorrow.

# Spiritual Initiative

People might say
    "You lack initiative."
To initiate,
    To begin anything
    Takes starting power.
I link initiative with drive.
    Push, pull, and
    Faster paced.
Could I initiate a new plan
    Of spiritual change?
Initiate the quiet mind.
The vastness
    Of doing nothing
    Is fertile ground
    For invention.
The rest initiative
    Is a radical
    Spiritual directive.
It gives rise to dreaming.

The garden initiative:

    A bold multi-dimensional plan

    Creates beauty

    Exercises the body

    And opens the door to

    The pleasure of the senses.

What could be more radical

    And fulfilling

    Than that?

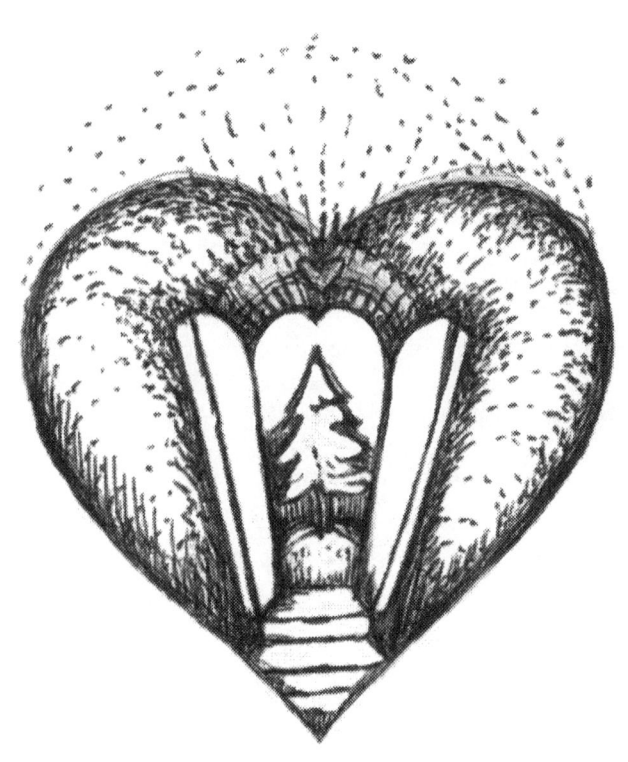

# Valentine Epiphany

I had an epiphany walking

across the street

from the ten minute jiffy lube garage.

I had a moment where my heart spoke

to the whole of me

and I heard, felt, knew

I loved myself.

Never, never, have I thought such a thing before.

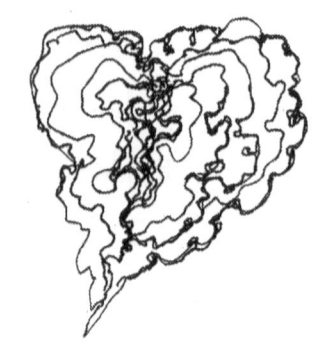

What happened in that second

as I crossed the street?

Drop by drop by drop,

the accumulation of grace filled my cup.

I saw no flashing wonders.

It was a quiet enlightenment

   an experience of gratitude

        infused each cell of my body.

        Gratitude overflowed

        onto the pavement.

Gratitude for having
had the chance to know myself,
to love myself.
for even just a few moments.

My Prayer:
May all beings enjoy
such a moment.
At least once in their lives.
May It Be So.
Amen,
the Heart.

What lights the candle in your heart?

What makes your heart feel like a marshmallow?

What turns you into a chocolate sundae?

# Tenderheart
## For Times of Vulnerability

"Don't give up hope!
In the universe of all possibilities
Miracles of loving
Can still occur."

# A Blessing for the New

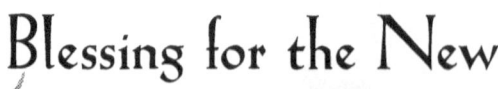

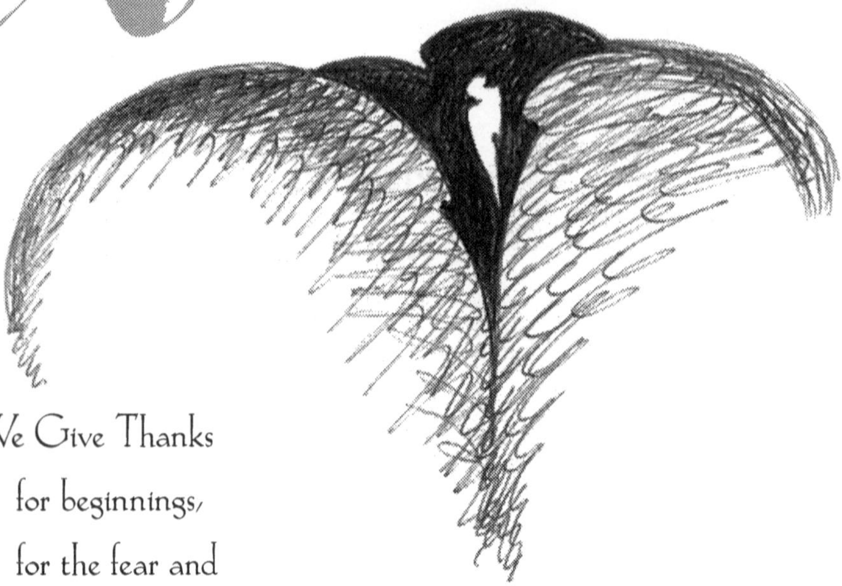

We Give Thanks
> for beginnings,
> for the fear and
> wonder
> of the new.

We ask a blessing on our intentions
> to Grow
>> in awe, which is both intimate and infinite.

Like a tiny seed gestating in the darkness
> pushing at the edges of becoming,
>> like the fiery birth of a star in a spiraling cosmos.

We ask a blessing on our impatience
> that we would learn the nature of Grace,

that we would gain tolerance for unknowing.
That we would evolve into kind witnesses
     of our own transformations
          and the transformations of others.


We ask a blessing for our gifts,
     that our talents known and unknown
          would more fully emerge,
          would be valued and affirmed,
          would be of service and be more fully integrated
          into our lives and our communities.


We ask that the sharing of our gifts be a source
     of joy and delight,
          renewal and refreshment
               to ourselves and those our lives might touch.


We ask that we might be blessed with
     courage and compassion which is the
          blossoming of the heart.

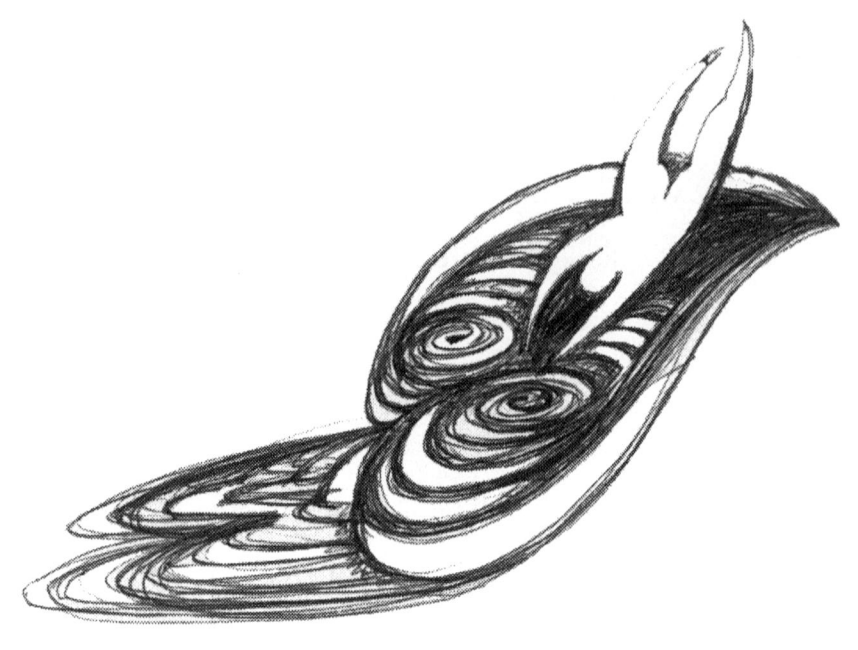

We ask that we would be blessed
 with the healing of our wounds,
  and we pray for healing for those we have wounded
   may we be blessed with self awareness, love and friendship.

May our souls be tuned
 so that we might lift up our voices and sing
  out of the darkness,
   out of the seed of the newness,
    the chrysalis emerging.

May we recognize ourselves
    as lilies, butterflies, ever-changing as the sea,
        a mirror for others, and the place to look to find
            our true nature.

May our questions become friends and guides,
    may we find comfort and creativity in quiet.

May we grow in clarity as we walk this path
    so that we might recognize and encounter
        the Divine in each breath
            and in each step.

# Beloved

Under your steady gaze
    and sure hand
      my heart is growing.
Against my best intentions
    I can't help loving you.

Its not the flaming, falling
    inferno of love.
      that is not the Divine prescription
    for my heart.

God said, "attention, moderate exercise
and lots of TLC."
What I now know is not romantic love
    it is real love.
The daily bread and communion.

# Cultivate my Soul

I give thanks for the outer fence
Around my fragile plants and flowers.

I give thanks for the outer fence.
The outer fence is a reminder
That the inner fence
Around my heart
Is softening and melting.

Do I still need
    The iron bars and
    Locks and keys
    To protect the inner garden?

Oh Beloved!
Cultivate my Soul.
　Handle this bruised bulb gently
That I might yet, under your sure pruning
　Gain new strength
To flower once again.

# Open the Door Oh, Beloved

Somewhere between
My head and my feet
A door is opening,
A lock unbolting.
In quiet awe
A new green shoot
Appears out of
rich black soil.
The act of planting seeds
Is ever
An act of faith.
Don't give up hope!
In the universe of all possibilities
Miracles of loving
Can still occur.

# Blessed ♥ Teacher

Guide me into delight,

Hold my fragile heart

In your most able hands.

You are with me

In the faces all around me.

You have embodied yourself

In every being I encounter.

Help me

To recognize you in all things.

Let it be

so.

How can I keep my heart open when I am afraid?

Can I treat myself gently?

Can you treat me tenderly?

# The Healing Power of Pets

"You touch us
With your wings and tails and soft noses
in the places of the soul
where no laughter is ever heard."

# For the Blessing of Pets
## A Prayer of Thanks

I give thanks for the blessing of pets.

    I give thanks for the heart opened

        by a delicate tongue

        washing superb whiskers.

I give thanks for my soul,

    blown open in all its shut places

    by your pink paws on my arm

    by your soft fur and purr sheltered next to me.

I give thanks for your solid affection that keeps you

waiting for my return each night.

As small as you are,

    a mouse

    a turtle, or finch

    or snowy cockatoo

you are companions of magnitude

you touch us

with your wings and tails and soft noses

in the places of the soul where no laughter

    is ever heard.

You touch us

  and tickle us

  and heal our wounds

  and when you die we grieve a death in the family.

Oh thank you Source of Creation for having

blessed us beyond words of thanks.

We thank you for the Blessings

of these dear creatures

  who live in the home

  of our hearts.

# Angels in Disguise

Angels do not come to us
Dressed in heavenly attire,
White wings gently flapping
The air about them scented
With lavender and myrrh.

Angels of consolation are shy.
They come to us in disguise
Dressed in dog-suits,
They sit on our laps
And absorb our tears
With soft and receptive ears.
Never capable of judgment
They offer us absolution
With their perfect love
And deeply silent eyes.

Angels come to us
Disguised as kittens
To restore our innocence,
To teach us to laugh again.
They re-member us
And re-knit our hearts,
Singing us into dreams
With purring lullabies.

Look,
There is an Angel
Disguised as a Buddha-cat
Sitting for hours
On top of the refrigerator.
The length of tails and whiskers
Is in direct proportion
To the measure
Of angel wings.

He or she
Who bathes your tired feet and hands
With a humble, raspy tongue
Is the faithful guardian angel
    Of your heart.
Do not be fooled
By fur, or fleas.

# In Praise Of
## My Most Purr-fect Teacher

My cat, always seeking the highest ground,
finds her perfect resting-place
atop the carved red lacquer
Tibetan altar.

Reclining like the Buddha she takes her rest
on the woven wool blanket which covers this station of prayer.
She is my purr-fect teacher.

"When you play,
Nothing exists but the contemplation
of the object of the moment."

Ball, bell, piece of fur, all become ritual objects.
    She embraces them in kitty mudras.
She stretches herself in a backward arching circle,
    tail touches ear in a yoga posture of grace.

She purrs a mantric syllable with half closed eyes.
    "When I sleep I surrender,
    and when I awake,
    I am totally present to each moment."

Kitty Dharma is most powerful.
    Therefore I offer thanks and praise to
        my most purr-fect teacher,
        who eats her kibble with gusto
        and releases the past into sleep
with twitching
outstretched paws
    atop the carved
        Tibetan altar.

# Meditation on Emptiness
## Given by the Feline Buddha-Fou

I sit before the empty bowl

　with one-pointed concentration.

I meditate on the void.

　I meditate on emptiness.

I sit without moving.

　I do not blink my eyes.

I keep my posture erect.

　My eyes are downcast.

I contemplate the void.

　I do not lift a paw.

I do not move a whisker.

　My tail retains a subtle curve.

I sit in silent focus.

　The bowl is form

　the interior space

　the void

　is emptiness.

Without effort on my part

　the void is filled

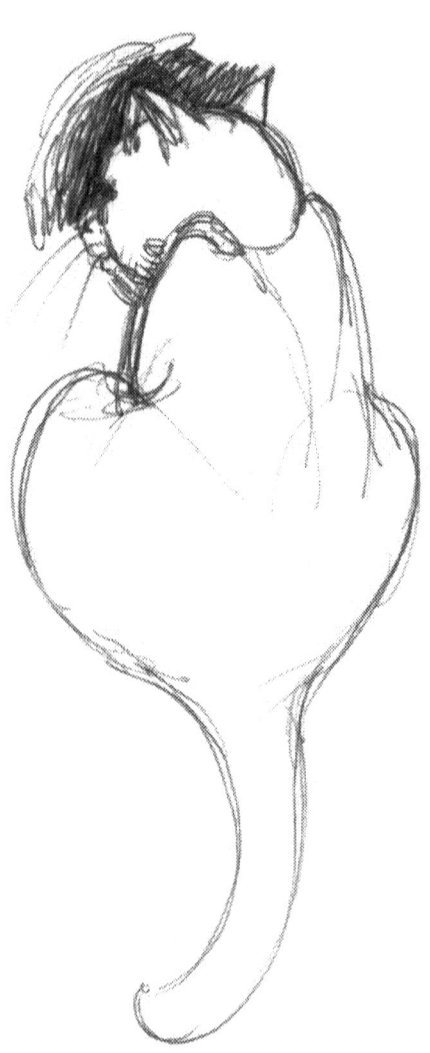

with small pieces of

salmon and cheese

bits of dried lamb and water.

The void is filled with

all that is needed

for my growth and health

in direct response to my meditation.

Created by

one-pointed contemplation

the void is filled without any effort

on my part.

The void is filled.

I partake

and then

the void is empty.

Meditation on the void

produces fulfilling results,

but

do not become attached

to the contents.

It is only in emptiness

That fullness can arise.

# The Sorrow of Loneliness

Loneliness is the curse of incarnation.

　　Oh, Creator of the Universe!

You who have given form to all things,

　　How did I end up

In this middle-aged

　　Single woman body?

All around me are beautiful others

　　Beautiful, single women and men.

We weep on our cats and

　　Our dogs become our comforters.

There is too much pain and sorrow

　　In this lonely life.

I have such compassion

　　For the sorrow of loneliness.

You have created us for partnership

　　And communion

But sadly,

　　I am giving up hope.

Hear my prayer,

　　Let the cries of the un-beloved

　　Come to you.

I want someone to love me
Like I love my cat.

# I Want Someone to Love Me
# Like I love my Cat

Dedicated to all the single people living with
their cats, dogs and other animal companions.


I want someone who will love me

    As I love my cat,

    Who loves me more as I age

    And adores my soft belly.

I want someone who doesn't mind

My periodic whining.
Who hears the need and fear
Beneath the offensive voice.
Responds with soft holding,
   "Oh, I hear you need snuggling!
   A thousand kisses upon your head.
   Of course you need salmon.
   Right away, this minute!
   You need space
   To be left alone or
   To go out."
Send me someone who responds
   To my pathetic
   Non-verbal mewings
And still, and still
   LOVES ME
   Always and completely.


Send me someone who is flexible.
   I never tire of watching my cat
   Roll herself into
   Ecstatic, yoga postures of delight.
   She is the master of flexibility,

She is the master of my heart
    For over a decade
    (at least 70 human years).
We never married,
    But my cat has taken me for better
    And certainly for worse.
I am looking for someone
    Cozy, and relaxed,
    Not brain-dead and passive.
Oh God, spare me from the
    Emotionally needy
    And financially impoverished!
Oh Holy One,
    Forgive my sin of cynicism.
Last week I contemplated a relationship
    And had a sign appear on my heart.
    It said
    "Unsafe at any speed!"

I need someone who brings me gifts
    Of value,
My cat
    Brings me gifts.

A pile of feathers appears
On my doorstep.


I love her clear boundaries
And respect her wishes.
She says:
"Don't hold me now"

or

"Not so tight.
I'll sleep with you tonight,
Or not."
I don't question her every mood.
I don't heap guilt on myself,
Or
If I do, I don't
Take it out on her.
Instead I bring her toys and treats
And think of ways to win her affections.
When she sleeps next to me
I feel blessed.
When she yawns at me
In the morning,
Breathing cat breath on my face,

I find it endearing, not gross.

Hear my plea and send me someone like that.

    We live well

    Side by side,

    In the same small house

    For longer than most of

    The human relationships

    I know.

My cat likes to sit in my favorite chair.

    Hair covers everything.

    Particularly my favorite black velvet pants.

Messes are left here and there

    And I clean up after with out complaint.

    Send me someone like that.

What about play and fun?

    My cat likes all my favorite movies.

    We watch them over and over again.

    We eat popcorn in bed,

    And sleep through the boring parts.

Send me someone who can be quiet with me

    In the garden,

    Walking between the flowers,

Sitting in the sun,

Contemplating the sprouts.

I'll pass on someone who catches

Beetles and eats them with relish.

Send me someone I can pray and meditate with,

In the morning, afternoon or evening.

We paws and give thanks

We sit in silence,

Together, attentive but not touching.

Just breathing and watching each other.

My cat is always patient with my busyness

But will demand that I leave the computer

To go to bed,

Snoring in front of me,

I long to bury my face in soft fur

And kiss the pad of each paw

And venerate every whisker.

But I will resist the temptation to

Awaken the sleeping beauty and

Interrupt the sleep of the beloved.

Please hear the prayers of all the lonely hearts

And send us

Someone that loves us like we love our cats.

# A Eulogy for the Life of Cisco Smith

We give thanks for the life of Cisco Smith,

Prince, among Cats.

Cisco, during your time on Earth

You raised the bar on the standards of being.

Not just for being an exemplar of felines,

Oh no, you taught us what it meant to embody the

BEST OF TRUE BEING FOR ALL SPECIES!!

You were ever the true and gentle soul,

A Buddha of equanimity

A territorial diplomat, easing all tension

Your kind presence was appreciated

By all who knew you.

Oh Gentle Man of fur.

We count ourselves lucky to have known you

We count ourselves fortunate to have shared your days.

As you come to the end of your time

Inhabiting this cat body,

There are no doubts in my mind as to the goodness of your soul.

I pray that you know how well you have been loved.

I selfishly pray

That your soul may return to earth some day

As a conscious leader of humans.


I know that any leader possessing your kind skills of being,

Offers hope to human kind.

If your soul is diffused into the cosmos

I pray that some of your gentle and diplomatic essence

Will take up residence in the hearts of world leaders,

And Light their way.


What a task I ask of you great soul.

Let your tired cat body rest now

As we fed you tuna and yogurt

We had the privilege to serve

Buddha and the Christ.

We were almost fooled by your disguise, as a cat.

We give thanks for blessing our hearts and lives

With your presence.

Amen, Be at Peace. Thank You.

Do you tie your heart into knots?

# Meditations for the Heart

"Forgiveness is a balm
To heal the broken heart
Patience is the physician
of the soul."

# Three Meditations
## On the Heart of Transformation

## 1

## Through the Fire

Once I had a dream
of leading a mission
on horseback
to rescue the abused children.

With children sitting in front
and children hanging on from behind
the only way home
was through a wall of flame.

Oh, the brave ponies,
they were angels
with their hooves on fire,
carrying us to safety.

Why are some of us condemned
to go through fire?
Is the word condemned
a judgment?
Or are we blessed
by the presence of
unrecognized Angels
hovering
in the center of combustion?

These angels say:
"You can take
the long slow road home
or,
take the path of fire."

As we tremble with fear
we can miss their promise
"We will hold you
so that you can open up your eyes
and view the beauty of the flames."

# 2

## Know the Fire

This is what I know of fire
    as a potter
    I made my life
    forming vessels
    out of pure white porcelain.
I would center a lump of clay
    and shape it as a cup
    or bowl, or vase
    until I had a form that
    would satisfy my eye.
To make my efforts function
    as a chalice for wine,
    or a plate to hold
    the meal,
Each and every individual piece
    had to be surrendered to the fire,
bricked into the cremation chamber.
The pot died to its old life

as water and silica

the ancient dried powder of stardust

from which we too are made.

There in the fire.

　And

ONLY IN THE FIRE

can transformation take place!

In the fire

　molecules are bonded, and fused.

In the fire, a new life takes place,

　a life of function happens

　in the fire.

That which was fluid

　becomes capable of holding the fluid.

Now, new from the fire,

　becomes the life of function.

Celebration, of holding the wine

　serving, and nurturing

　so, what is the message of the transformed clay?

Surrender to the fire,

　　bathe in the fire,

　　dance and sit,

　　meditate and sing to the fire.

Do not let your fear hurry you.

Rest in the center

　　of the flaming lotus of change.

Crack open your chest.

Call the fire in

　　yelling I am the fire woman

　　burning from the inside out.

# 3

# The Transforming Power of Fire

For a year
I gave a daily prayer
of thanks.
Writing slowly
the practice of gratitude.
I knew a man
    who daily wrote
    his sins
    and burned the book
    at the turning of the year.
The leaves of the burnt book
    turned back and each page
    became the petal of a black rose
    that lay upon the altar
    as an offering
    to the transforming power of the fire.

# A Prayer For Beginning the Day

A Prayer for Right Speech.
A Blessing to Soften the Heart and Tongue.

You who gave the geese their voices
    to call to one another over miles,
    through wind and storms,
you who gave the dolphin and whale
their most elegant songs.

We call on you to soften our hearts and tongues
    and guide our words.

Lead us into right speech,
so that communications between us may promote
    understanding, mutual respect and
    freedom from limiting language
    which has held us in bondage to
    old structures and definitions.
To ascend,
to spread our wings,

Help us to hear one another,
Calling to one another,
Encouraging one another,
    ourselves and others.

to ride the wind, and experience the heights
    to take the risks of
        exploring the depths of our souls.

Help us to rise up singing
    our most elegant songs of connection,
        liberation and praise.
            Hear our prayers for right speech
                and bless our hearts and tongues,
                    Amen.

# To Heal the Broken Heart

I have some good news and
I have some bad news.

Bad news first.
Not all broken hearts can be cured
How can you be cured
From the death of your mother?
Or the loss of your lover?

Physicians can cure the leaky valve, but
There is no cure for life.

Now the good news.
Healing can always occur.
Healing can transform
Those last days and moments
When death is inevitable
Into ecstatic communion with
Kin and cosmos.

Healing can transform
The worm of cancer
Into the butterfly of spirit.

Healing can occur.
The miracle of metamorphosis
Has scientific proof.

Foul green caterpillars
Devouring the garden
Turning green leaves
And tomatoes into pulp
Turn into monarchs.

I have seen the silver cocoons
Dangling from the drain spout.
I have seen the butterflies
Fanning their new wings,
Black and gold
On the milkweed blossoms,

In the late autumn afternoon
Before beginning their migration south.


Just because we can't see them
After they set sail
For the warm coast of Rio
Doesn't mean they don't exist
Bringing smiles
To the faces of the Samba dancers.


Do we try to cure the caterpillars?
Perhaps healing for the heart
Means accepting the inevitability of change.
Even becoming a butterfly
Might be a frightening concept,
To some caterpillars.


Yes,
Here is the good news
Healing can alter
The garden variety monsters
Of anger, and resentment
Into Luna Moths

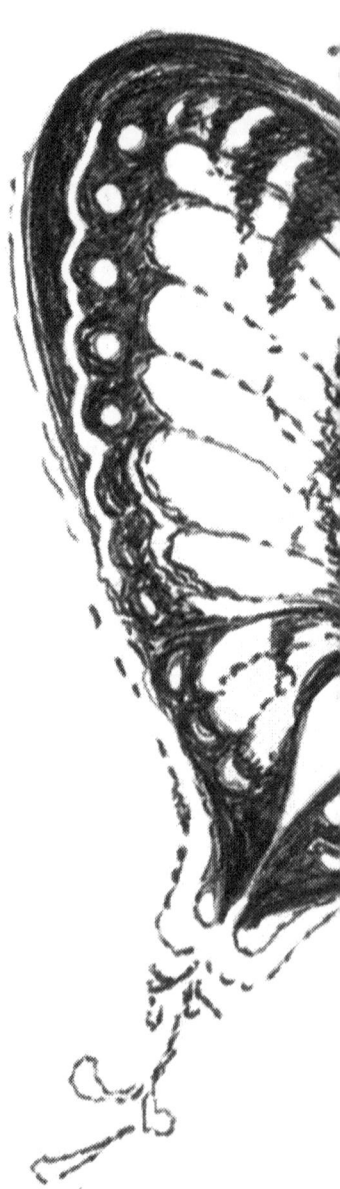

Of forgiveness, and patience
(not to be confused with Patient!!)
Forgiveness is a balm
To heal the broken heart.
Patience is the physician
Of the soul.

# A Prayer for Times of Impatience and Frustration

Oh Lord, I lift up my impatience and frustration to you,
transform the energy of these emotions.
I am powerless in the face of these irritations.

Teach me the power of grace so that I may
grow in patience and tolerance,
illuminate the areas of my life
where I feel inadequate
and unable to change.
Re-create me as a magnifying glass
so that I may perceive your presence
in my life and recognize you
even in the things I find annoying.
Shine through me with your transforming radiance
and in this light
purify the obstacles of stubbornness
that stand in the way of growth.

Please work with me.

Even in my pettiness

　　do not abandon me

　　but help grow me up

　　so that I may fulfill the purpose of my being

　　which I would appreciate your revealing to me sooner

　　rather than later!

# Solstice Prayer

Oh Bright Spirit,
   Infuse our darkness
With your light

In every particle
   Of sorrow
Illuminate our despair

In every cell
    Of loneliness
    Ignite awareness
Of connection to the cosmos.

Oh Bright Spirit,
    Enlighten our hearts
With Divine and human love.

Create in us
    An incandescent soul
    Of compassion
That will not be extinguished,

But which will join
    Heart to heart
    Until the universe
Is kindled
    With the blessed
    Flame of Peace.

# A Prayer For Reconnection to the Cosmos and Creation

From a sense of isolation

I offer a prayer for reconnection to the cosmos and creation.

In my dreams, waking or sleeping

Let me rise up on a glowing spiral to the stars,

Let the light pour in

Let my molecules and atoms be infused with light

And let me be dispersed like phosphorescence on the wake

Of a dolphins tail, on the edge of a wave.

Let my phosphorescent particles dissipate into the darkness

Let me float peacefully as part of a vast and breathing sea.

Oh great mother owl

Who hovers over us, and in the darkness,

Sees the bits and pieces that we are,

Sweep my particles back together from the surface of the sea

From the edges of the universe, from the Milky Way

From where I am lost.

Gather the bits of me back together

under your huge soft cloud wings

And re-knit me into your body.

Sooth my fears with your soft feathers.

Clutch my heart with your talons

and even in pain remind my heart

To beat again in rhythm with creation.

Can I breathe the universe into my heart?

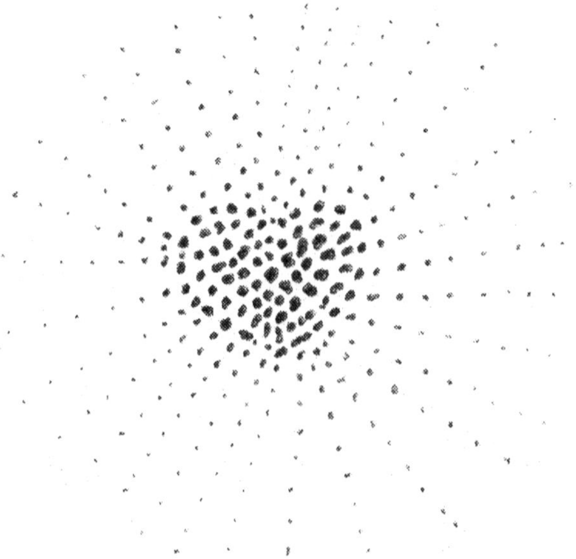

www.ingramcontent.com/pod-product-compliance
Lightning Source LLC
Chambersburg PA
CBHW052147170626
46812CB00004B/1622